THE GURDJIEFF PUZZLE – NOW

THE GURDJIEFF PUZZLE
NOW

TALKS ON TRANSFORMATION

by

Terje Tonne

Compiled by Robert Moses

Gateways Books, Nevada City

Published by Gateways Books and Tapes
P.O. Box 370
Nevada City, CA 95959
www.gatewaysbooksandtapes.com
(530) 477-8101

First published in a hardcover edition in 2001
by Den Norske Gurdjieff Stiftelsen
in co-operation with Eureka Editions, Utrecht, The Netherlands
www.gurdjieff-oslo.no

Cover design: iTRANSmedia
Cover photo: "Difficult Road" by Carl Bernhard Beck

Library of Congress Cataloging-in-Publication data:
Tonne, Terje, 1951-
The Gurdjieff puzzle now : talks on transformation / by Terje Tonne ;
compiled by Robert Moses.
p. cm.
Includes bibliographical references.
ISBN-10: 90-72395-41-7 (hardcover)
ISBN-13: 978-0-89556-165-7 (softcover)
ISBN-10: 0-89556-165-4 (softcover)
1. Fourth Way (Occultism) 2. Gurdjieff, Georges Ivanovitch, 1872-
1949.
3. Uspenskii, P. D. (Petr Dem'ianovich), 1878-1947. 4. Nicoll, Maurice,
1884-1953. 5. Pogson, Beryl, 1895- Work life. I. Moses, Robert, 1966-
II. Title.
BP605.G92T66 2006
197--dc22
2006019369

Dedicated to
Mr. George Cornelius

A link between
Heaven and Earth

This book is for people already familiar with the Work Ideas of the Fourth Way as presented by Gurdjieff, Ouspensky and Maurice Nicoll, and therefore there is no explanation of the terms used. For background information please refer to *In Search of The Miraculous* by P. D. Ouspensky or additional sources of information listed at the back of this book.

CONTENTS

FOREWORD

This work is very simple. It is so simple that our minds, being used to the complexities of modern life and its corresponding forms of thinking, have difficulties believing that the truth is actually lying there before our very eyes. Through trying to reach the truth, we discover that there is a price tag attached to it: the simple task of reaching one's inner reality means going through a forest of *unreality* in order to pay for it. At first we go steadily forward and then we get lost. Then we start to recognize where we are, but lose our way time after time and have to start reading the map anew. We *fall* and have a difficult time rising back up again and continuing on our path. A number of strange creatures appear, trying to persuade us to go back and forget the whole thing. "There is nothing behind those trees," they say. "Behind that hill there is another hill. Are you sure you want to go there?" As we continue our journey we sometimes "think" that they are right. So we start to believe in them, doubting our task and forgetting our aim. It did seem so clear and simple once—so right and obvious. Wasn't it just to follow these signs?

In the story of *Peer Gynt*, the protagonist believes in the voices of the different creatures he meets. He is led far away from his home and the woman who truly loves him, Solveig. (The name Solveig literally means "sunway" in Norwegian.) When Peer returns to her after a life of inner betrayal, he asks her if he ever was *himself*, if he was ever true to his real, inner man. She answers, "Yes, in my faith, in my hope and in my love." She represents a sacred place in Peer Gynt and a deeper place within ourselves. In the Fourth Way we are told that our true self isn't lost, it is we who are lost—lost in the imaginary, the superficial and habitually acquired traits of our outer psychology. What is true and real can never be lost. It is we who can lose touch with it. It is there all the time, like Solveig, waiting for us to return—in touch with her faith and hoping for our arrival as she patiently watches us wander about in our unrealized lives.

So in our bewildered state, in our forest of fake, the guide shows us the way out of the bog gradually, pointing here and there. Having walked before us, he anticipates our complaints, our confusion and our suffering. But he cannot do the hard work for us. This we must do for ourselves. We do discover that there *is* another hill behind that hill, and that it may be this way for the rest of the journey. It is our way of coping with this reality that has to change. *Then* we catch a glimpse of the meaning of the phrase "accepting our limitations means breaking our limitations."

The words and phrases in this book grow out of an atmosphere in which an experience has taken place. This is where meaning exists—in the experience of discovering what *is*. Books like this one can be helpful for this reason. Although words alone are empty, we have a teaching that encourages us to get to the meaning behind the words and to that still place that gave birth to them. This oral teaching is a means to return there when we find ourselves drifting away.

The words you will find here come from someone who has paid a price, again and again, to be able to speak them. Often we have found ourselves trying to share what can't be explained—we have an insight and it provides new meanings that give rise to questions that we didn't know we had. And out of our confusion, when we are receptive, he supports us as we go towards a silence that can inform. From his experience of what is the right fuel for the return journey to ourselves, he asks us to come half way to his promptings. Entering this atmosphere is only part of the effort. To live more *in* this atmosphere means to see our non-being as a doorway, to accept ourselves as we are and to just be.

Being in a school offers the experience of being in the care of a guide. Our guide knows us well and pays a great price in and for his own life to be able to offer us the thorough, individual help that's needed to wake up. The mystery of the experience of receiving this help is not readily understood by our ordinary minds. In addition, receiving this gift orally is neither easy nor comfortable. It is in this atmosphere where we hope to find, with the help of his suggestions, our own direction in the creation of our inner lives. To find out what is useless and useful for our return journey is why we have listened to and collected these words.

The contents of this direct gift are scattered throughout what you have in your hands right now. As words they can only vaguely convey bits and pieces of the atmosphere of someone who knows the way home.

Some of the sections of this book are taken from the manuscript entitled *The Theory of Objective Art.*

Birgit Holmsen
Robert Moses
January 24, 2001

AUTHOR'S PREFACE

This book is a product of a journey, one which has not exactly followed a straight line. It has included some dead ends and getting lost a few times in my attempts to put the Gurdjieff work into practise. For those of you new to Gurdjieff and his work (perhaps, even, to this journey) and/or unacquainted with group work, I would like to pass on a few words about the practice of this work within a group context and some advice based on my experience of over 25 years. In order to become more familiar with Gurdjieff's ideas you can look at the books in the selected bibliography in the back of the book.

Although I think that it is true that reading a book about the Gurdjieff work can be good preparation, practising it must be done within a group. The reason is simple—without guidance one can deceive oneself and continue to visit the same blind alleys that one has always travelled along. This work is about learning how not to do that.

So, how to find a group that really works? This is a very difficult question that can only be answered through experience. There are, though, signs to look out for that can warn you when you yourself meet a group. Some of these are: an elitist attitude ("we are the only true interpreters of his word"), playing the money game, and separatism ("we are the only ones with the rights to practice these methods").

Members of a true group, including the guide, must always be ready to question themselves and be prepared not to support attitudes that allow the feeling that one has reached a certain level of being and does not have to try so much anymore. The Gurdjieff work is not to make one comfortable and complacent. The work is a living entity, and so is a group. It operates within cosmic laws like everything else that is alive.

Within group work there is room for regular exercises, exchanging observations and practicing the Movements. Taking part in these helps us to show the truth about who we think we are, but are not, so that we can nourish a more real part of ourselves and gradually realise the potential we have within us, as all human beings have, to serve a higher level in the universe. We experience that we do not have to live a purely biological life tied to the needs of our planetary body. Group work is of indescribable value because, in a practical way, it puts man's potential for development into a larger context in which the concept of individuality takes on another meaning.

But, ultimately, participation in group work has to come down to a personal need to deal with the life we are given for it to be effective. Gurdjieff's work can only help us when questions like "Who am I?" or "What am I doing on this planet?" are living ones.

When I came in contact with this work, I intuitively knew there was something of great value in it. To someone new to this work I would say that the most important thing of all is to build on this by never giving up—to try to turn in the direction of your own heart. Your own sincerity will always guide you in terms of what is necessary and what is not. Something else that has helped me was that right from the beginning I have tried to follow an inner conviction that there is a meaning to life and that it is available. Along the way I have seen that this meaning can only be revealed through a non-stop, continuous journey.

Somehow my need has attracted help as I have gone along, such as in meeting Mr. George Cornelius, and this kind of help has been fundamental in building a bridge between a conviction present in me as a child and the potential of my future. Hopefully you will find something in this book that resonates with something real within yourself and that can be of help in solidifying the steps you have already taken or in supporting you during the ones to come.

—Terje Tonne
Oslo, Norway, November 2005

SINCERITY

We must have a wish that has no motives outside itself.

The depths of self-observation can be measured by your ability to be sincere.

When you catch a glimpse of a weakness, accept it. Then it is more possible to see how dumb it is.

A real worker cannot allow himself to become a spiritual aristocrat. He must first prepare, and then be ready to question himself and the quality of his wish to work, over and over again.

Let the exercise come to me. Try not to try too hard. Thinking I can do disturbs the silence. The principle of, "Man cannot do," is forgotten. Ego tries to do—it is often the Ego that wants to succeed and to do the exercise. *Why* do we want to do the exercise?

There is a tendency to keep oneself down (through speaking negatively about oneself) because the machine associates it with honesty. In a way it is right to say that honesty puts your weaknesses on the table, but it doesn't always work the other way around. We simply have too many buffers that deny us the chance for not defending ourselves if we find ourselves in the awkward position of being caught with our pants down. Nothing real can come from an emotional feature.

Most people behave "in an ordinary way" because they do not know they exist and do not remember themselves. Some, still "ordinary," but with the feeling of being "extraordinary," pretend to remember themselves. Try to do the right thing for the right reason—remember yourself and stay ordinary.

When we compare ourselves to others, there is always an aspect of self-love. Either we complain for not being the same or one easily becomes a "swagger." Some sticks have two dead ends, unfortunately.

The only thing that can break down buffers is sincerity.

"I's" that are opposed to the work always have excellent excuses. How can we see through them, if not through that special sensitivity that springs from sincerity?

To look from the source of your attention will be to know that you know that you are. But now, how close can you get?

NEED

We need need, then wish, then some understanding, then right method and then help.

Hopelessness is not a starting point. Helplessness is a good one, often perfect.

If you don't need this work, it can't help you.

HUMILITY

Between the objective necessity and the wish lies the personal need for help.

Paying back even a little from the great wealth we receive from esoteric teaching bypasses self-importance and breeds humility.

The work—it isn't so much about what I've accomplished, but a deeper recognition of what I lack. You know...the one who is smart is stupid; the one who knows he is stupid is smart.

SELF-OBSERVATION

Self-observation is collecting facts. To wish to work with what you have seen is a different area. In between them is the deep, disturbing recognition of the lack of unity.

Self-observation is often to recognize that things aren't what they seem to be.

During self-observation we reveal what we are not and then we have to learn how to stay with what is left.

If sharing an observation with the group is useful for someone else, then it is useful for you. We must learn to speak with more intention and be able to listen to ourselves.

Q: How to separate and then take care of what has been observed?

A: The lower wants to reduce the higher's meaning. Through an uncritical use of symbols meaning can easily be lost and we are left in darkness or a blindness. Symbols don't always carry information in such a practical sense. A reduction from the meaning of an original experience may lead to self-deception. Are we not often ready, too ready, to believe in a representation, a symbol? It gives us such an easy access to belief.

In the first kind of self-observation we observe the functioning of the machine, most often the characteristics of the wrong functions of centres. When we recognize that we share these wrong functions with others, that they also have them, this kind of observation can lead us towards a wish not to judge.

Deeper self-observation has to include our chief feature, the part in us that makes us deceive ourselves through avoiding necessary suffering. There is a fence. On one side of it I don't ask myself why I'm not working on myself. On the other side of this fence I am open to this question and in this place this question is of importance to me. This openness is already present within the process of passing over it.

The upper part of the first kind of self-observation, or the lower part of the second kind, can bring us to the realisation that all of the efforts that have been made don't fully bring us to what we came here for.

FALSE PERSONALITY

False personality does not like ascending octaves because they start with a passive DO.

Intellectual ability should be a servant for higher worlds and not as it most often is, an ornament of false personality. If it is not misused it leads to intelligence.

To stand face to face, in periods, with the lack of motivation, it is necessary to reconnect to the truth through sincerity. This must be the basis for all real inner movement. If we let ourselves have a blind spot with regard to our motivation, we end up allowing ourselves to slip back and become more and more involved in activities of non-sense. Spiritual aristocrats always have a blind spot that, wherever it is revealed, is forced, through facts, by its own limitations to show its actual face—vanity. But the question remains...is there a wish within me to see?

Self-blame is incompatible with inner-transformation.

We live in a cage made up of mental and emotional bars, placed in a wall-less room. As time goes by, if false personality plays an active part, these bars become gradually fixed and the possibility for change diminishes as one approaches the state of psychological death.

Thinking about being in harmony is such a pleasant thought, but working for it might seem like a nightmare.

Many questions disappear when you enter the realm of reality. One is "Does God exist?" Such questions are not real. They are always related to some form of self-importance, like, "*I* believe." or "*I* don't."

DEMANDS

When you are small, making demands is part of your language. But when you get older the demand is made on you not to make demands on others, but to create your own life.

Expectations stand in the way of being in the moment. We must not demand certain answers. There is a difference between wishing for something and demanding it.

False personality often demands to be entertained.

Inner accounts often presuppose the imagined idea that justice exists in the world.

PAYMENT

What does it mean to pay? To pay means to have a wish and an aim, to be patient and to suffer. To gain the currency of ability through self-observation and through this gather material to see which way you want to go. The only way is to pay in advance. You put the money on the table, and you let it go. You might not get the goods for years. *But you will get your goods; no one or nothing can deny you what you have paid for.* It is a cosmic principle.

False Personality always uses a credit card; it never pays in cash.

A basis for a real motive must always be based in the wish for truth.

Relax emotions through the intellect. "What kind of quality can I expect out of being worried? Where will it bring me at the best? Am I satisfied with this?...and where it's bringing me?" Then comes understanding—from working—and within that understanding, relax.

We have to work all the time; when we are in an amusement park, when we win the big Teddy Bear, etc., etc., etc. You know, ordinary situations.

EFFORT

A challenge without obstacles is unthinkable.

We must try from the right place, instead of trying "to do"—let the work come to us.

The word "effort" is easily associated with unpleasant-ness, but opening oneself to the question "Do I real-ly know what effort means?" can arouse a certain kind of curiosity which is not so easily associated with meaninglessness. On the contrary, what is the mean-ing of effort?

Relax and sense your body form the corner of your eye. That's a work "I". See?

Deputy Steward only starts working in moments of effort. Deputy Steward is effort.

Big efforts, small area—results.
Big efforts, big area—often fails.

You have to make your aim as practical as the resist-ance seems. The hope is lying in the fact that the resistance is not what it seems.

The worst days are often the best. We need the good

days to prepare for them and we need the worst days to prepare ourselves to die in the right way.

There are reactions to reactions, often called efforts.

Not to identify is very, very difficult, almost impossible. But it is possible. If we don't have something in us that says it is possible, then we can't continue to work.

When it really counts, and it does all the time, but we don't understand that it does, we're not in the danger zone called sinning. But when we have some understanding and don't make effort, we are sinners.

Q: How can I keep continuity in my inner work?

A: Is there an effort that you do not yet know of? One that can fit into either the First, Second or Third line of work, and why not all of them?

Try not to identify with physical pain. You are not the pain, but you have a machine that sends pain. But you must **work** for not identifying with the pain. Make the effort of dividing your attention over and over again.

There's only one thing you don't need to rest from, and that's the work. You can have real rest only when you work on yourself. So, take a break. If you can, take five.

CHOICE

In situations when your mechanics are pulling you in different directions, stand in front of them as if you had a choice. When we practice this over a long enough time, we gradually create two things: energy and an ability to do.

When your weakness is producing resistance, it can be a good sign. Then you know that you are tracking it down. Stand in front of it as if you have a choice and say, "Hello. Thank you. Goodbye."

The potentiality to choose is within our human nature, but a machine has no choice.

WILL

When, through effort, all the centres pull in the same direction, we can receive a taste of will.

Will is connected to suffering. It is based on intention, guided by the inner voice, travelling along on the refined energy of understanding for the necessity of suffering.

You have to wish to see and see to will.

SUFFERING

Q: How can I get rid of fear?

A: Do you want to get rid of fear, or do you want to work with it? If you want to get rid of it, then get yourself a buffer—another one—just add to it. If you want to *work* with it then let the fear be there, don't say no to it. Within the experience of *accepting* difficulties is the key to what you are looking for.

Intentional suffering means to accept yourself and others —now.

Refuse to believe and be brought away by irritation, physical discomfort, indignation or any other means that the machine might use to continue its terrorism. I will not sympathise with my machine while it is in its reactional patterns. I will refuse very quietly.

Awakening is connected to unpleasantness. The suffering of seeing how it really looks and not fighting it, but bearing it, is unavoidable in order to wake up. We must realise that the rules for real living are unchangeable, but acceptable.

Intentional suffering is to accept that which is to be done. Goliath kept David on the job. He wasn't unemployed!

Sorrow is never "weighty." Unnecessary suffering is one-sided. It has only a bitter taste. Sorrow is bitter-sweet. It is the formatory apparatus that questions the lightness in sorrow. It expects a lop-sided experience.

Look out for the mechanics that make it difficult to make the effort of allowing suffering. Let unnecessary suffering go. I must breathe out in order to be able to breathe in.

In order to suffer we must be sincere.

Intentional suffering is the condition for contacting that which is behind the mechanical.

Two signs of unnecessary suffering:
    1. It often has an element of blame,
    2. It can never be transformed—that is, unless its meaningless is recognised.

Q: What does "The one who sleeps doesn't sin" mean?

A: Sinning is not a conscious action. It's a pull towards a lower world within oneself when one part has a certain awareness of a wrong direction. It's not an action in accordance with a higher world. Expanding your consciousness, seeing, realising all produce, due to their nature, the consequence of obligation. If we see and don't take upon ourselves the consequences of what we see but let ourselves drift into a lower world of indifference, self-pity, irritation or any other denying factors, then the question of sin comes up. Justification is correcting things in our minds. But we don't want that. We want to pay our debts and stand in front of our own reality, and suffer for our shortcomings and make mistakes so that we can move once more.

Try for a period, as an experiment, to forget success and failure, forget payment. It is too easily associated with reward. Forget right and wrong. Did you make a fool of yourself? Let's say you did, look at it as only a fact, unconnected with good or bad, and from there go on.

"Do I suffer enough to understand who I am not?" This question will only be deeply experienced by a person who has a certain understanding of what is at stake here and is willing to pay the price for living in reality and not in a dream. Such a man has the conviction that anything outside reality is worth the deepest intentional suffering.

HELP

Real strength has to come from within you. You can receive help in recognising your potential strength through stillness.

Q: How can I be more motivated?

A: Motivation comes from an inner, disturbing cry. When you don't identify and see your limitations then the motivation can come. But from exactly where, we do not know.

When you are *in* the work, nothing is impossible to handle. It might be difficult, but you are not in a hopeless situation.

We always get help when we ask for it, if we really need it. But the expectations of false personality are not met due to the fact that we often ask for help when we do not need it.

We must enter a meeting from below. It's not intelligent to enter a meeting as a champion of the universe.

Higher forces will never authorise you to blame yourself. Be present and co-operate with them. Self-blame is vanity.

ATTENTION

Attention is energy, a force that can be used. This great gift is a latent ability in us all that we must be more and ever more receptive to through our own efforts. It has been given, but it must also be received.

When you stand in front of a situation, direct your attention and expand your awareness – include more and more. And try not to interfere with this process, then you will experience that there are no walls, only thresholds. This ability has no direction; it has all directions.

You have to engage your attention; it is there. But you have to direct it so that you become *aware*. Otherwise all the "I's" will come and start the show. Remember what Robert De Ropp said, "You can have a candle without having a flame but you cannot have a flame without a candle." Engage your attention! Look out the window, listen, or ask if anyone needs anything. Sense your body. Do. Don't be done with.

A justifying "I" is like a thief in the night with a crowbar. When a spotlight, that is attention, is directed at him, he is frozen in place and he finds it very awkward to move. And with still more attention he sooner or later cracks, just like the Norwegian trolls do when the sun is coming up.

When you direct attention on small "I's", they become less active. In fact, their last activity is leaving.

When attention is scattered, the intellectual centre runs around in circles. Instead of taking in impressions, we associate. The old tape is running. This is what we generally call our "thoughts." These nourish themselves from our energy reservoir. If you close down the supply of this energy through directed attention, these tapes will slow down and eventually become manageable.

External considering is only possible with directed attention. Without it, the best your behavioural patterns can do is act as if *that's* enough to enter the present moment! It's not a question of behaviour. It is a question of being.

The process of awakening is ruled by laws. They are constructed in such a way so that we can have a possibility to awaken *due to the fact that* we have limitations. By including our limitations in our experience, we make the experience meaning-full.

Increased awareness gives increased possibilities for knowing what the moment demands—or, if you like, needs.

Concentration is not a bad thing! It's just not the same as attention. You can verify this by concentrating your attention.

Either you take care of your attention or it will be raped in the red light district of your mind.

SHOCKS

We must not be concerned about what we have accomplished. We will have the opportunity of seeing that in the process of dying. Take that food away from self-love and let it accumulate on another scale.

A shock is never nice. It might prove useful. That's as close to nice as it can get.

A shock can be given, but it must also be received. This work is a shock in itself for those who wish to receive it.

SLEEP

Q: Why can a man not do?

A: In countless ways man is ignorant of fundamental laws. *One of which is that he doesn't calculate with resistance.* And his ignorance is upheld through justifications when things don't turn out as he desired. Or if it happens to do so, to go the way he desired, then his ignorance prevents him from seeing that it was an accident. So, he describes the accident as a quality of his ability to do. That's sleeping man turning in his circle.

To complain two times about the same coffee is a clear indication of sleep. Eventually one time will be *more* than enough. This is a slow process.

Interrupting while someone else is speaking is a manifestation of identification.

Judgment is a passivity clothed in activity.

When the going gets stupid, the stupid get going. (In reference to the comments made by the formatory apparatus.)

Rules are in a sense only for sleepwalkers.

Daydreaming—the aimless movements of thoughts wandering through the landscape of the past or future. It is careful in one sense only—to bypass the present moment.

Imagination is our tendency to avoid the moment by trying to look at it from a point in ourselves that does not exist.

Meaning already exists. We are, as it were, surrounded by it; but our attention is elsewhere.

LEARNING

What is the work? The clue is to experience every situation as food. And remember, reality does not serve food that is past its sell-by date.

We know something about what it is like to be quiet in the moving centre, and we know something about what it is like to be unquiet in the emotional centre. We must appreciate whatever we learn.

This work is about failing, but in the right way. After all, we are intensively instructed from our non-being.

To calculate with Second Force is to recognize the nature of our form of existence. One moment we see the diversity of "I's" in ourselves and then the next moment we forget about this and we are daydreaming. *This* is our nature. We must be able to calculate with Second Force and not lose hope. It is a labyrinth. It is difficult, but not impossible. Calculating with Second Force is to know this diversity and that our two-sidedness is a right starting point. "I's" that say it isn't possible are sleeping. We build slowly. In the mean time, don't lose hope.

To live from the work is to try again and again, not being depressed by our shortcomings, but by being informed and nourished by our non-being.

We are often helped by some kind of terror. When you really experience "the terror of the situation," that is, without identification, and you get thrown around, then you can experience an informative transparency, a state without buffers, where you surprisingly do not have a wish for something else other than your own realisation that "Man cannot do."

"Man cannot do," but we can learn to do....by not identifying with the fact that we cannot.

An esoteric school is a place where you can learn to get in touch with fundamental laws. Unless you are able to utilise the Law of Seven by bridging intervals with inner dimensions, you will be lost at your moment of death.

New qualities and a new sensitivity must always be in relation to the authority that comes from a need or a necessity.

Q: How can I work in moments where interest seems to slip away?

A: Are you interested in taking responsibility for your own indifference?

It isn't impossible, but it appears impossible because it's close to impossible. Helplessness and hopelessness are two different things.

Except for unnecessary suffering—the *only* thing you can lose by separating from a mood—moods can be separated from without loss.

On one level, to ponder is the intellectual part of the emotional centre's ability to wonder about the ideas and your own existence.

What we receive in the work are tools to enter the moment. In the moment there is never anything to be afraid of, not even suffering.

Q: What does trust mean?

A: Become aware of what you can't trust in yourself and have trust in your recognition, and hold onto it. Remember Rodney Collin's words, "affirm, affirm, affirm."

To move in the work is to become less predictable and more accountable.

An intelligent attitude towards the limitations of subjective morals will paralyse them. In fact, they'd be paralysed by their own stupidity. Flexibility and movement, that's work.

The only way to have stability in this work is to be able to change when circumstances change, without changing. That is, not to react to changes but to include them into an ever enlarging acceptance. *An ever enlarg-*

ing I that is growing through diminishing the reactional self.

The best way to prepare to correct things is not in correcting them, but seeing more of what needs to be corrected. There is a time for everything.

Elegance + substance = strength. We have to be able to work in different ways. Sometimes like the bull and sometimes like the bullfighter. Freedom is the ability to adjust effort to the needs of the moment. Generally, we try to adjust the moment to the limit of our dislike for making efforts....which, by the way, is never elegant.

Work is to learn to eat things we haven't eaten before.

Try to find out what it means to *not* sleep instead of searching for what it means to awaken.

We are so used to thinking that there is a solution in an answer. But at a certain stage it is necessary to ask a question without desiring, demanding or hoping for an answer. By sticking to the question and making it more and more pure, we can limit the area of chief feature. Beyond a real, pure question, there is always an answer coming from something that is more intelligent than the functioning of our minds.

Satisfaction always gives rise to dissatisfaction. We have

to come to terms with the laws. Have a calculating attitude and include the pull towards dissatisfaction. It is all within a process from which we can learn.

Q: How to work on correcting and justifying?

A: Make effort to stay in the body. Don't identify when there is failure, but quickly forgive yourself.

You can't listen to your heart or your body in your head.

Pondering is an activity outside the function of thinking.

Q: Who is doing the pondering?

A: Yes, *that's* the question. It's definitely not an "I" residing in the intellectual centre. If it is, it is not pondering; it's simply one "I" inhabiting the intellectual centre thinking of another "I", or even thinking that it ponders.

Q: Is it the Master who can ponder?

A: That's too far away; we have to ponder from a level within reach, for example Deputy Steward and Steward. You can only ponder from that place within yourself where you can be honest. In pondering we are open to what has been, what will be and what is. Pondering is watching with the deepest interest that part of everything which is happening to pass through the tunnel of the present moment. I must do it with all of me—my heart, my body. And with the most independent part of the intellect.

On a larger scale there is no room for the misunderstanding that First, Second and Third lines of work are separate entities. The substance of all real work is for the unity of all—independent of its form.

EMOTIONS

Listen to your heart, not your head. The depth of this can be recognised when you see that your head has led you astray, or better, when your heart has saved you.

A real emotion never associates to anything outside itself.

With a balanced emotional centre one can receive emotions that come from higher parts. When the emotional centre is unbalanced, there is simply too much noise to hear them.

The machine may display some kind of emotions and call it "conscience." The deceptiveness of these reactional emotions lies in their speed—their intensity. We easily become impressed because they are so intense. But remember, the quality of a guitarist is not necessarily measured by the speed of his fingers.

There is a difference between a light heart and heart-lite.

BUFFERS

Try to see the buffer from two sides. It can bring you to sleep or you could wake up in the recognition of it.

That which sees and doesn't comment can use a weakness as a vehicle to penetrate more deeply into the situation I'm in. Silence is such an informer.

Buffers keep us from realising the truth about ourselves. There are buffers in each centre. A buffer can only be removed by will. Those in the emotional centre appear very quickly. Start with the buffers in the moving centre. Don't try to change everything at once, but take the pain, the friction to see them.

To work on buffers in the moving centre will help you to realise something about openness and how to work on the buffers in the other centres.

To hurry in connection with having forgotten something is more often a buffer for seeing that one was not present than to eliminate, for a practical reason, the time one has lost. It's a manifestation of inner considering in the moving centre.

One way to work on buffers in the emotional and intellectual centre can be not to express an opinion when it is not necessary to speak. When we allow ourselves to be open instead of reacting to criticism, there is a silent moment when we don't know exactly what to do, although we know we don't want to go with the pull. When we are mechanical there is no question about it, we think we know what to do and feel we have the right to.

Be open to why you behave in a certain way. Then your buffers will be revealed to you.

In the stew called false personality, the main ingredients are features and buffers. Did you ever think about getting out of that pot and not letting the kitchen cross your mind?

A feature is a son of a buffer.

Buffers prepare the ground for features.

What often happens when we only have a vague wish to work is that we later correct with the intellectual centre by saying, "I should have done it differently," instead of accepting. This is a buffer. We must try to avoid going into the trap of non-suffering.

Buffers are lies that justify the behaviour of a feature.

Q: How can I learn to play a role?

A: How can you possibly play a role until you have seen your buffers?

WISH

We might not succeed in trying, but we don't have to lose our wish to try again. It's simply not intelligent.

When a desire becomes influenced by something higher than a function then it becomes a wish.

The power of wish is indescribable.

REDUCTION

Everything is an explanation in itself, like a real relationship. And it can't be explained, because how can you explain an explanation without losing it?

When the intellect tries to grasp a situation, it reduces the existing moment to an abstract concept. The map is never the same as the landscape. When we stand in front of a situation, our machine habitually categorises the impression through a reduction-filter based on former recordings that are similar or vaguely similar. The consequences of this filter are that we do not relate directly to our experiences, but with what we associate them with.

A real reduction always brings a new meaning.

IDENTIFICATION

Objective enthusiasm is aiming at what one is enthusiastic about while subjective enthusiasm is a paralysing drug.

"What on Earth is going on?" That's interest. "What the Hell is going on?" That's identification.

If you don't want to be identified with the impressions that come, then you have to be there to guide them through.

Money is just money. It is only your attitude to it that makes it something else. Here it is important to have a negative attitude towards your own identification. But money is just money.

You will be stronger each time you can stand in front of your weaknesses without identifying with them. This is a law that nothing can change.

ENERGY

Energy—don't be so concerned about making it; try not to pour it out. Try to understand people. Then you will not so easily be threatened by that in you which wants to complain about them.

Not to identify means taking care of the energy you have, creating energy and allowing your energy to flow freely. Identification is one of the most meaningless activities we can engage in. To understand this is to understand a meaning behind the word "tragedy."

The energy necessary for making a decision must be extracted from necessary suffering and transformed through intentional suffering.

FRICTION

When life is unpleasant, it is not the exception. It is the rule. It is a part of this form of existence. Some get a lot of it, others get less. Why this form of existence has, on a larger scale, this *form* we do not know. It's none of our business. But in its form lies the keyhole to our inner freedom. The key is divided attention.

(In answer to a question.) There will always be resistance. Why it is like this, why the law of three, we don't know. We only know that it is like this, although in the Ray of Creation you can find out how the eternal movement is set in motion. The possibilities you get are limited to a certain number. Do you want to use those possibilities?

Our tendency to correct is not something to run away from but something to face.

Peace and quiet inside has to embrace the shaking so that it can't be shook off. Shaking can't shake the shaking off.

The more difficult the situation, the larger the contrast between mechanicalness and peace inside.

For weak people, the work ideas will shatter their self-picture just when they receive friction. When you see this and you can't help them, remember: no judgments or demands. Just quietly realise this and move on. There is no room for sentimentality in this work.

A school of harmony tries to place emphasis on harmonising with the difficulties we receive instead of creating additional ones. The method of friction is always the same but the vehicle changes, depending on the cosmic need of the period and on the essential temperament of the one conducting the school.

Discover associations. Don't manifest them through talking. Replace the "satisfaction" of manifesting them and the dissatisfaction when not allowing yourself to manifest them with the satisfaction of knowing yourself.

If you stick to the work, also in difficult times, it is guaranteed that you will come out the other side differently than you had imagined. Remember the saying, "It is when it is getting steep that you are moving upwards."

PATIENCE

True patience is to stand in front of your own moment and to know that there is a time for everything. All that we can wish for is here. There's a moment in this moment. It's your moment. Don't ask why.

Patience is beyond impatience. It is an ability to be, to dwell in the moment, and not be taken by a reactional "I" that's not accepting the situation. We are not as patient as we would like to think. We nourish this picture of ourselves by recognising that we are not impatient when others are but we don't register that others aren't when we are.

When patience is not connected with a will based on real values, then "patience" is simply a reaction of the machine. Patience is a result of initiative based on an intention. Acceptance is to relate to what I'm impatient about – what I usually run away from. There is always an aspect of accepting in the activity of being patient. Hidden within impatience you can always find the lack of ability to accept.

STILLNESS

This is friendly advice. Not much can be said about stillness, but we are going to stress the idea of being still.

Silence isn't something you do, it is something you receive.

When you experience freedom, there are no words for it, because you are not in associations. It's simply "I am." Such moments can give inspiration. They have to become a source for motivation through recognising that they are scarce and that they are what I wish for in order for them to be of further practical value.

When we truly sense our bodies, it is a form of prayer.

When we have a quiet mind, we can't have inner accounts.

That which boasts the least has the greatest reason to do so. But it doesn't... it becomes quiet in its own totality.

One quiet moment connects with another and after awhile the distance between them gets smaller. Being still is moving in reality. Have a look at your resistance from out of the corner of your eye.

When you are confused, sit down in three centres until the fog lifts. Deep understanding is not thinking, but feeling what you see through all of your impressions in the moment.

Consciousness is often mistaken for and regarded as an activity in the mind. This is not so. Consciousness is a certain state of awareness where we recognize, for example, mind activities, emotional moods, the physical sensation of our bodies, who we are and what we want without being attached. It is attached only to the experience. It is a state beyond words, images and definitions. The more we speak about it, the less we speak about it.

When I'm in a silent place, I see from being that which *isn't* through the commenting it makes—usually my feeling of "I" is connected to this non-being. That which can bring us into being we don't want to remove by way of correcting. With a right attitude obstacles can become opportunity.

In silence the one who serves is the one who eats.

Pondering is not bringing things together in your mind. It is more like allowing the experience of the question of living not to be held back by the thinking.

Silence is an activity, a very quiet one. You can do things that don't interfere with the silence. A role player can't play a role without it.

REALITY

Again we start with separating. Separate from the mechanical feeling of "I". Don't identify. Keep floating. Nothing that is real ever stops. What we need inside is a good coating of psychological Teflon. What is this?

No great thinker is thinking very much. He recognises things as they are.

Although there is nothing ordinary in the cosmic, there is nothing unordinary about the cosmic. You see, we are right in the midst of a mystery. It is our attitude that makes it only ordinary. It is only in the state of presence that we can recognize how extraordinary the ordinary is.

Invite your nagging "I's" to come in and have a cup of coffee! Then they will say, "We don't feel like coffee right now...." And then they'll run away. Now you can see who they are. They never bother to roll up their sleeves and join in on your inner work. They won't stay for anything, not even for coffee.

To love your mother and father on a higher scale is to love World 12 and World 6. The same laws apply to different levels.

The problematic nature of illusion is that it is dressed up as reality.

⚜

CENTRES

When your intellectual centre is over-involved in relaxing the moving centre, the result is always tension. Relaxing the body must be done in the body, just as you can't play tennis from the spectator's seats.

Look at your intellectual centre as a knife that you carry in a sheath. When there is a need for it then take it out in silence, use it and after that put it back into the sheath.

To give energy to the centres by acknowledging them—that is, not ignoring them—will be to work in a relaxed manner without the immediate danger of losing energy. Enthusiasm renders us liable to be more involved in the process of recognising our centre and in not failing in our task than in more fully recognizing the centres in action. We can be so occupied with the function of our intellectual centre that we don't know what we are thinking about.

There *is* attention in second state, but it wanders around like a fish in a bowl, undirected. Now here. Now there. There must be attention in lower parts of centres. How could something that doesn't exist do such a thing as wander?

When I'm really in three centres I gain access for a moment to the impossibility of identifying with negativity.

Try to move intentionally. That would be to activate the inner part of the moving centre. The inner part of the moving centre has the capacity to lead you to the other intellectual parts of the centres. Try.

It is a help to practise inner silence when other people address you. Inner silence is not necessarily dependent on the functioning of the centres, although there has to be some kind of balance. You can't wait until it's perfect and then start with the exercise. If, for example, there is an uneasiness in the emotional centre, this can be difficult to stop, but inner silence can still be practised regardless because it comes from consciousness.

HARMONY

We can't correct, repair, adjust or fix our mental situation mentally. It must be a cooperation between all centres.

Thoughts are one type of substance; emotions are another type of substance. Different parts of the apparatus run on different types of substances. That which directs attention on the apparatus uses a finer substance. That which makes an inner decision uses an even finer substance. Try now and then to experience these substances separately. Through separation they will eventually blend harmoniously together.

Student: What is the sign of Man No.4?
Guide: What happens to a punching ball when you hit it?
Student: It comes back to its original position.
Guide: That's correct.
Student: What is the sign of Man No.4 who is close to No.5?
Guide: He comes back very quickly to his original position.

Man No. 1, 2 and 3 are hit and handled. Man No.4 is hit and reminded to try to cope with the situation.

Q: How to get into balance?

A: Make room for reality within through being sincere. Then the truth about the situation you are in will reveal itself to you and connect with the rest of reality. There can only be one reality. If there were two, one would limit the other in its being real. This is even true so far down as the level of logic. The truth comes down from such a high place and it keeps gaining momentum on its way. That's one of the reasons why it can penetrate down to lower levels—where it can easily turn into a phrase.

When you connect with the present moment, it's got everything you need. It gives itself to everyone, like air, without question.

When we have stabilised at a certain level, then a limitation will become a definite possibility.

Symmetry in an object can thus represent two sides living in harmony and balance with each other, like a dying man recognising that death is a part of living. When symmetry, in an almost limitless variety of ways, is manifested in life apart from an understanding of its origin, it must be because the source of the form contains so much harmony in itself and also that man is so much in need of it. Consciousness is to know what we need.

The balance and order of physical life is amazing. Amongst a vast variety of temperatures existing in the universe, the temperature on the planet Earth is designed in such a way that it allows plants, animals and man to exist. The recognition of this fact can open the door to wonder. Variations of temperature are one of the innumerable cooperating forces that are in action to provide the existence of life on our planet. A parallel is found in the basic elements in the structure of music—rhythm and pause, life itself being the tone.

FEAR

Q: How can I work with fear?

A: Look at your fear with interest instead of having a negative attitude toward it. Is there anything there that you can use, anything that you can work with? This creates acceptance and a wish to learn. What more could you ask for?

That which tries too hard is often based on a doubt about one's possibilities. It has to be observed that doubts are a form of fear in the emotional centre. Seeing beyond fear requires awareness and makes more awareness. One has no right to deprive oneself of an opportunity before one has tried.

The only thing to be afraid of is not discovering that there is nothing to be afraid of. There is nothing to be afraid of.

Emotional fear—do as the wine tasters do. Have a sip. Taste it. Taste it again and spit it out. Swallow that.

ACCEPTANCE

When the fine energy of acceptance comes, then the heart is filled.

Student: Inner talking, how can I stop it?
Guide: Do you want to stop it or put an end to it? If you want to stop it, it will make an end of you. If you want to make an end to it, accept it and you will stop it. You see, things are not what we think they are. We don't try to stop a lorry in the middle of the road in our own mind, but try to attack it from the hillside with a psychology of attention. We also have to step aside from our inner road named desire.

Sometimes just a small desire to change the situation will ruin its possibilities. You can't really want another situation until you have accepted the one you have.

You have to recognize your situation—do you think this is informative?

All work for acceptance always starts with accepting yourself.

To accept actively means to connect your acceptance to your aim. Don't forget, passive acceptance is often a buffer.

We must play with the cards we have instead of reacting against them from our centre of gravity and social background.

Try to stand in front of your dislikes and likes ... without associations ... and see what happens.

Real fear has a fairness about it.

Accepting your limitations is breaking your limitations.

It is not intelligent to question from an attitude. It is wiser to accept the attitude.

Let reality hit me so much that I won't be surprised when death comes.

DOORS

Once you know where you lose yourself, you know where to find yourself.

You cannot find the solution if you don't know what the problem is.

Within an open attitude towards your hindrance lies the key. Openness opens.

We can't open the new door with the old key.

You can't get out, but you can get in.

To let go is to let the walls of fear disappear. After all, there are no walls in the doorway.

Work memory says, "In this room is a door."

All starting points have two surfaces: one turning upwards, because one's possibilities are recognised, and one facing downwards because one sees one's limitations only as a limiting factor. A door has two adjoining rooms.

Not ever to let go is as close as Man No. 4 can get to reality.

We can extract an extraordinary strength from ordinary situations when we are not identifying with them.

It isn't necessarily such a big difference between the ordinary and the miraculous. The difference can only be when you are not there. *Be* in an ordinary situation and experience the miraculous.

When you know how to enter the present moment you will find that there is no queuing up at the gate. The boarding is immediate. And the plane goes in all directions.

Leaving stupidity and entering intelligence is a very quiet process.

The New Man will outlive your body. You came with no body and you *might* leave with no body. That is, if you work on yourself and can learn to *be* somebody.

The Fourth Way is a long short cut into oneself.

When you are dead, you can't sit here (said while driving).

To sense the body is an essential activity. Defining the sensations belongs to personality. So stay with the experience.

The best meetings are not the ones you get a hold of, but that get a hold of you.

You came to find yourself, but what I hope you experience is losing yourself.

EXPERIENCE

Everything in nature, except for Man, is given an integrated function that it is intended to fulfil. Man must create a function in himself. What is my function? Already with this question self-love can sneak in. Try to differentiate between "What is *my* role?" and "What is my *role*?" What is my obligation as a human being? There is a limit to the guide's role. Your final information has to come from inside you.

Q: What is meaning?

A: No.

Q: What?

A: Wrong question. Where is meaning? You see? ...Meaning is in the present moment. So, the right question is, "How do I get there?" Oh, I'm sorry, "Here."

Real thoughts originate from experiences of the present moment. Then there is no difference between *that* thought and being.

To be is a definite, indefinable state.

Hidden outside what the eye can tell me by mere looking; what the ear can convey by simple hearing; the nose by receiving any odour; or the tongue by tasting, lies that which pulls me away from the impressions. An object can speak to us directly within the experience of simple awareness. A landscape can hit us with itself. A smell can penetrate us by its very nature. A sound can echo sound. Any intellectual interpretation will fail in its attempt to convey meaning and will distort the transformational ability possessed by awareness because it is based on a reflection of an experience and not the mere experience itself.

We must not doubt in the name of the work what we have actually experienced. Formatory mind operates on the currency of a two-sided coin. But you can only buy something of value with a one-sided coin. "Man cannot do," but he can learn to through bringing opposites together. When you don't see a limitation as a dead-end, but as a possibility—a reminding factor— then the coin turns into a sphere. You can flip a coin but not a sphere.

OBSTACLES

Confusion is often a state which false personality uses in order to control the situation.

Striving might diminish your possibilities.

The highest form of logic reveals its own limitations.

We don't want to look backwards, only forwards. You wouldn't drive a car that way. It's dangerous. Same laws, different levels.

Q: I have observed that I swing between worry and being cheerful. How do I get into balance?

A: Certain things are difficult. Can you try actively not to worry by including your worry into your experience? When you are not identified with worry, it is often because you are identified with something else, like being cheerful, and not because you are remembering not to worry.

To enter the present moment, you have to pull the door towards yourself. The door opens towards you, not out. So first you have to clean up the room you are in.

As long as the space inside is filled with weaknesses

and self-importance, there cannot be room to be present and to do what you have to do there—namely, to respond to reality, or if you like, to be responsible.

When things are difficult and you are identified with meaninglessness, then try to remember that it isn't meaning that has left you. It is you that has left meaning.

PROCESSES

The right relation between work and method can be illustrated in the triad of healing—Matter, Form, Life. Work does not come from method, but method springs from the wish to work. So, when you are negative, sense your body and experience life. Identification with methods and work ideas will bring you to the triad of corruption—Form, Life, Matter—where one's behavioural patterns try to fake the results that can only come from the experience of being alive.

The whole process of transformation is a message. The separate particles in the stream rarely carry a clearly recognisable message.

Identification with identification is corruption. When the attention is totally sucked into second force, there can be no change. Identification functioning as a reminding factor is a part of the triad of regeneration.

Carbon dioxide and imagination are different forms of excrement. Imagination is a mental excrement. If we don't get rid of waste products then we will become poisoned. Keep breathing.

Obstructing one's life and the life of the school with one's own negative manifestations is like clogging the pipe that higher influence can flow through. Being identified with a closed section of the pipe is a form of doubt towards oneself, one's worthiness of receiving and transmitting influences and lack of valuation of those influences that seek to heal and put things in order. To accept the flow is to accept oneself and vice versa. We have to deal with our attitudes; otherwise our attitudes will deal with us.

VALUATION

You must find something in yourself that you respect. Find one small thing. Remember where you came from and why you are here. What you have been given is what you need.

To value suffering is to see that it is a privilege—a blessing to be here. To really see a limitation is to enjoy the possibility it brings. We have to wake up through some means! Remember the uninterested one, Peer Gynt, in one of his reactions he says something in the nature of when something tastes bad, one has to spit and hope for the power of habit.

You don't have to create values, you have to work to be able to recognize them—and then you can penetrate some of the aspects of Kundabuffer.

We must not try to define experience. By defining experiences we are tearing apart meaning.

To appreciate a fire is so much more difficult than to dislike the cold.

GETTING BEYOND ONESELF

Failure is not failure. It is a new opportunity. That's a positive attitude.

Q: What does it mean to approach eternity by seeing "three or more things in succession?"

A: Let's start with what we have—"three," and consider that this "three" was chosen intelligently.

Q: Three forces?

A: When we stand in front of a difficulty we have the possibility of dealing with it. Mechanicalness might creep up on us through imagination about what it would be like if we succeeded or the mechanical imagination within Second Force of how we might fail. (Remember that if you are deep enough in Second Force you won't even receive help when it is given.) The Third Force will be something which is completely new and different—even different than what we can imagine in the first place. The imagination within First Force and the imagination within Second Force will fight each other through trying to exclude one another. Third Force has a different quality—the quality of including. Whatever difficulty we have, when we truly work with it, contains within it a possibility for transformation. When a particular situation, any situation, is in front of us, it always has something in common with all other situations and it is not limited; for example, to the immediate expectations we may have of the situation that we're in. The possibility of resolving a situation shares something, something fundamental, with what we may call all possible opportunities. Any situation has more in it than we can expect to see at first glance. When you reach a state of freedom through separation it doesn't matter whether you had freed yourself through non-identification with time, desire, doubt or some other kind of evil. But what counts is that which is beyond all these elements of sleep. There is a state available to a man which can't be changed and is, so to speak, independent of the means that brought him to this state. An opportunity reached through work is the same as all other opportunities. Ouspensky said, "Eternity is the infinite existence of every moment of time." This is material for pondering.

To act our life, not to be acted upon. That's the question.

Try to see things on a larger scale. This work is not for personal development. Individual work exists because there is a cosmic need. When you work in this way you move towards invisibility.

Chief feature has a tendency to compare itself to others. It attempts the impossible. There will always be someone better or worse, but we cannot become someone else. We can only change through trying the possible.

Be thankful for your weaknesses. Without them you would be in a labyrinth without an exit.

Do not think about your weaknesses and don't think about separating from them. Separate from them. No work can be in the head only. At the best, your head can be a supporter.

Q: What is self-observation?

A: To collect facts. Deeper self-observation is the ability to see what you are missing.

Q: How can I work on my weakness of arguing?

A: Try to give to others something other than what you see you lack. A form for external considering is to give room to another person. The essential self has nothing against this. It is false personality that can't manage it. So, one must move in oneself.

A true emotion is connected with the action of going beyond an emotional reaction.

A self-realised man must listen to everything... including others.

Subjective thinking makes it so that you always want to

understand in order to remove the uncertainty. When you take away the uncertainty, you take away the necessity of subjective thinking. The present moment has everything in it and it manifests through being certain that you are. All other certainties become secondary to it. When uncertainties are removed from their dominant and active position then you gradually destroy the necessity for subjective thinking.

Rarely can we see the co-operation of stubbornness and stupidity as clearly as when "ourself" prevents us from coming to ourself. It is only an experience of that we are not what we think we are that can make us realize that we cannot lose something we don't have.

Unnecessary pressure brings you down. Right pressure can't bring you down, it brings you up. Recognize the unnecessary pressure and embrace the unavoidable. Try to keep the door unlocked.

Make an effort not to be so certain that you can't be open. Openness begins where certainty ends. A deeper certainty starts whenever and wherever openness proceeds.

When you begin to see yourself through feelings, you see what you are like from the inside out. You begin to understand why you look the way you do on the outside. In World 24 your external manifestation of your curiosity to life... real life, corresponds with your feeling of yourself. The reason why this might tilt your brain is because you haven't tilted it intentionally.

What you need to do is tilt your acquired side, render it passive, so that the real side can be left, and then only be together with itself in its wholeness. This is real self-love. When you experience that your external side reflects the moment itself, you will see that outside time you have always looked the same. It is all one.

QUANTITY/QUALITY

It is not a question of how big or how "strong" a lie is. It is a question of lying or not lying, because when we lie, we lose contact with reality.

A harmonious co-operation between volume and quality would be to use a lot of money in the right way.

The reduction of art into an historical element always carries the danger of taking away from the importance of the contents and stressing its manifestation of form in time. Sacred art, containing an aspect of timelessness in itself by its very nature, is therefore particularly vulnerable to this method of contemporary art history. Art forms which live and die under the laws of fashion, *tres chic et passé*, are in less danger due to the fact that they are firmly anchored in the external manifestations of their own time. They are unable to be affected by a timelessness that the moment is always a part of. It can't lose a thing it doesn't have. We are so accustomed to regard quality as identical with volume that we can lose our potential for wisdom in a large volume of accumulated knowledge that's found through analysis. The motive of knowledge is often based on the weakness called power.

Part-time workers expect full-time pay. But part-time workers never get paid at all. It's all or nothing.

SELF-REMEMBERING

Q: Is self-remembering always the same?

A: It is always a new door, but to the same room.

We must take off everything that isn't us in order to return. The beginning of self-remembering is to disconnect rather than to connect, and from there we will reconnect.

There is freedom in being like the blue cloudless sky. But we must seek freedom in being that sky when there are clouds.

To work on three lines simultaneously is a situation springing from the relationship between the experience and the awareness of it.

Deep joy is simply to know and feel together—to be in touch with consciousness and conscience.

Let the contradictions come and don't run away. Continue to stay.

Try not to exclude anything. Include, include. Because when you include everything, what is not **real** will exclude itself.

When we live in remembrance of ourselves, we accept what is given to us, and in that way live in correspondence with our task in life. As a result, we will project harmony.

Often the last real thought, in the process of entering inner silence, is that there isn't much to think about.

PRESENCE

You can lose, but you can't win. You can only let the presence win.

(On a trip in the North of Norway, said while driving) What you can hope to find in a good book are indications of what you can find in this curve. What you can hope to find in an excellent book are indications of how you can find what is in this curve.

If you are present to disturbances, external or internal, they can't destroy you.

A real moment is always the same moment.

Q: I used to have an experience more often but now I often worry. I have seen that I worry about losing my thread. How can I continue from where I once was?

A: The work can't be done through the head. This approach always leads to fear and worry and worry and fear. Don't be afraid of losing an experience. Let it loose and allow it to return to where it came from. It will find its own way home. But try to find *your* way back, which is always the present moment. Then your former understanding will receive you quietly as you enter.

The illusion of time comes out of the mind's structure

of time and this is based on the senses. Try to think of something in light of the past or the imagined future. Then let the details go. Just exist... All you can have is the child of now. Everything else is a lie.

When you think unnecessary thoughts it brings you to an unnecessary place in yourself. But you always *are* in a necessary place. When you *think* you are in a necessary place when you are not, how can you be present? To fulfil the most necessary need is to realise that you always are in a necessary place, that is, to accept your own situation and be where you are.

The purpose of the body is to serve that which wishes to be present.

To be present is to taste the truth. The theories are a means for leading you to it. The theories aren't the experience of truth itself. If you ever wondered where you forget, this is it.

Guide: Is it more important to taste good wine than bad wine?
Student: Yes, uh...No!
Guide: What?
Student: No.

In deep presence the past becomes the present and the future becomes visible.

I would rather suffer in reality than be happy in a dream.

The experience of presence can't be associated with anything. It's difficult to know about a lot and know that you must rarely refer to it.

SECOND CONSCIOUS SHOCK

The work "I" performing the act of The Second Conscious Shock is a long-trained athlete, whose ability is not solely based on his own efforts. This ability is given through grace. Throughout his training he accumulates, first through grace and then effort, the conviction of his aim to awaken. His aim is initially conceived in the First Conscious Shock and he is still under its influence during the process of transforming negativity. Everything that is given must be received, and this athlete is a receiver.

ONE BODY

You cannot play a real role without having contact with a real part of yourself.

Humanity is one body.

You can make friends outside of time. You simply have to become someone they can trust—if you share their valuation and you are trustworthy.

OBJECTIVE ART

There is, and has always has been, an objective relationship between a man's level of being and the product of his actions. In the same way that a physically short person is unable to take an object off a shelf high above the ground, a person with a low being cannot create works of objective art. If man has a wish to change his level of being he must simply accept the situation he is in and begin from there. No other starting point exists, because a man's starting point is the sum of all the processes that have touched him until now.

In order to produce objective art, the artist has to know himself and be able to master the different functions given him—mind, heart and body—so as not to prevent the present moment and its energies from entering him.

One of the major characteristics of any artist is the underlying need for expression. But for the expression to be more than a mere reaction, it is necessary for him to develop an inner responsibility for being objective towards his reactions so that the original impression in itself can be digested and not merely function as a spring-board for a set of associations involuntarily programmed by former events.

Any purely intellectual viewpoint we may take towards objective art will fail because it cannot take itself into account as a limiting factor. It cannot, so to speak, take itself as seriously as reality demands in order to participate. Objective art, or the reception of it, is not a product of thinking but of experience.

Man's fundamental urge for identity makes him vulnerable to the results of entering and belonging to collective danger-zones. Art-styles, groups, schools or -isms of any kind function as very powerful means to support and sustain his subjectivity. As a part of the universe, man belongs already, but to this he is not awake.

The original form that Raphael imitated from Leonardo did not come from imitating a form but from a substance of being. Leonardo's form came from the substance of his presence. Leonardo Da Vinci recognised the necessity for inner struggle. In light of this, Raphael's activities might seem like a stroll in the park.

We are all familiar with vague comments such as, "It's life-like," when talking about a picture, sculpture or a piece of music. Although this comment might sometimes prove to lean in the right direction, it is somehow lacking contact with its foundation. The most sensible basis for such a statement is to be found in the experience of life itself for the person behind this statement. Only then will he have the material to recognize life, because life is always compatible with itself, independent of the form it takes. The problem is not so much that life, if it is there in an object, is hiding from man, as that man is hiding from his own experience of life.

We will never know how many doors have been closed to generations and generations of people through the blind acceptance of the authorised and academic history of art. But we can think of the idea of "the blind leading the blind" and that our possibility to break loose from that chain gang lies in our wish to work, according to principles more objective than the ones that make us bypass our own experience of existing in the moment.

Any theory on what art is or why art exists is powerless when it is not based on the original idea of beauty and harmony being a means for man to find the way back to himself and to his Real I, which is a part of everything, and the purpose of his own existence. The search is not one-sided. It also includes suffering, but an intelligent kind of suffering where its potential is actualised through the joy of sacrificing what one is not.

Tones that move you move your stillness.

Through the ages, one of man's activities has been to express and manifest something that he has come across out of necessity and then absorbed through study. The art of hunting is probably the first of all arts.

The esoteric meaning or origin of the harmony in symmetry in art can be seen as a wish to manifest the possibility for man to be able to correspond to objective reality.

The minor scale potentially carries within itself a balance of true sorrow and deeply felt meaning that's beyond thinking.

To be able to take in the impressions of the structure of nature and existence as they are, and not to stop them at the point where a fixed attitude inhibits one from passing through a door and entering wonder, is an art in itself—the art of living. This can provide an emotional understanding of all forms of art; the art of the heart reveals the heart of the art.

TWO DIFFERENT DIRECTIONS

Q: I would like to ask a question that is connected to a situation this afternoon. It is a situation that happens every now and then. My experience is that the pulse in my body rises even though I don't experience reactions to what I normally call stress. The exact situation was that we were sitting down to have dinner and then the neighbour rang the doorbell. He is helping us with some work on the outside of the house. It was absolutely necessary that he did the work right then and there. So I had to go outside and show him. Then we had only so much time to eat and then I had to drive my son to a sporting event before the meeting tonight and my husband had an appointment that I had to help him prepare for. It was these kinds of things. And what I experience is that it all goes around in my head. There are so many things to relate to and I know things aren't in order. When I had these moments of silence before the meeting, I realised there's an answer through setting time for finding the way back to stillness. And I wonder if there are ways... I wish to receive help to work with the situation then and there.

A: When we recognize that we have an experience of things not being in order... an uneasiness... but we know that there is something that we might be able to experience in another way through seeing it from the outside, then there can be seen something going in one direction and something going in another.

Is there anyone here, now, that experiences that what we are talking about now becomes less vague when you can take into account that there are these two directions?

The reason why I am speaking about this here and now is —when this happened to you then, there were these two directions potentially accessible. But you couldn't work with it then because you couldn't do anything else but what you were doing at that time. But what about right now? Can we experience that there is something on its way down, such as confusion, and that we are losing energy because of this and at the same time be in the actual experience of this actual situation? And have the feeling... receive... that this is not so hopeless. In fact, there is something happening. Can you stand on both sides of the fence?

So to be present means to be present to what is, to something that pulls us down and something that pulls us... away... another way. To stand in the middle of this, that is maybe what you can try next time... maybe? The former time is past. And this moment here is soon past, too.

So you asked for help to save energy? Next time, have attention on what pulls you down and the *reaction to it*. Just simply have attention on these two sides and be aware of them and see... feel it. And take it from there, without expecting a more concrete solution.

So, we settle for this, that we can become aware of the situation where these two things are happening at the same time. And that we try to have attention on both things at the same time. Can you take that? There exists the concept, identification... and then there is this; not to identify with any of them. And then we can see that what we tend to identify ourselves with is there... somewhere.

You can try to include into your octave of impressions what is happening inside. Also, these parts that pull you in different directions. At the same time you can have the impression of "I am moving in a different direction than *those*." Can you... or can we try to let all of the impressions that exist here and now, that is, the sum of them... be something that we can relate to? We are speaking about the impressions octave, etc... Yeah, but what can come of it? ... Very little... for all of us, as a rule, very little. And sometimes something, and rarely quite a lot, and sometimes surprisingly much, and so on. Isn't that true? ... but... Why does this octave of impressions stop? Well, we know we have attitudes. But then again, we let something slip through anyhow because we have this wish to be different, to live. And that which is the solution is to... or one solution is to take in as many impressions as possible. Take in impressions of that which is worried; include your worries in the impression octave. Include the tension in the body ... the impressions of them... Include?

Q: Mistakes?

A: Yes, very good, include that which we *call* mistakes and even that which *calls* something a mistake... an attitude. So that we can receive the sum of all that is there...then we are speaking of a quite different dimension. And in that dimension we are informed in quite a new way in regards to what it means to be present. A new quality of feeling... very fine energies: compact, but at the same time ethereal, lightness with direction, certainty. That is, what the experience is is valuation. Even about valuation we can *then* say a little about it... without speaking less and less about it. Something completely different takes place.

The sum of your experiences must not be hindered. It must be allowed to float freely... even to look at something that "I should have avoided"... "*This* I should not have done," "*This* I don't have to do," "*This* I will have to try," include these too. Include that which says "This I must try." That is, don't try that.

STOP... STOP... all of that. And *then* you start to move... all that we believed was a movement, for example in the form of, "This I will try to do." Stop... be present... and include that which says, "I will try to be present." Include the desire and the striving. Stop the striving to be present. BE present. Stop avoiding. When you stop on one level you start on another. But then again, you have to include as *much* as possible. That is, at the best, the sum of all your experiences. We stop ourselves by saying, "We shouldn't have done that"... *that's* not it.

So, include the tension and all that which you looked upon as a hindrance. Then the hindrances themselves start to be a solution... Is there something here? Is there something here alive for you? Self-pity, self-pity also has to be included, when self-pity comes. "Oh, how to get out of self-pity, I want to get out of self-pity, I want to avoid self-pity." Stop avoiding, stop striving. *Be* present. Let *all* of it come to your impression of yourself. Then you will see that there exist no hindrances... There are no hindrances... It's all there.

That's why in the same room somebody can be present. Same time, same room... they can use the room and the time to get out of time and into presence. While others in the same temperature, same room, same time, and with the same smell in the room, strain themselves in the struggle to be present or they are looking in each other's plastic bags to see what they have bought today. Ridiculous. It is available the whole time. There are no hindrances. We *believe* that there are hindrances. But that's not believing; that's a reaction. Meaning is here; it has never left. It is we who leave. We are not even doing the leaving.

TWO CUPS

A: There are two methods. You can sit down and be quiet so that something new can come in. The body is calm. The emotional centre becomes calm and then the head. One way or another sometimes you can come under an influence of calmness that can enter through the body. We are not going to go into details right now about how the head can be emptied. I will only say that it can't be done through thinking. Calm inside and empty head... The other method is built upon a new way of thinking. It demands that you become open to a new way of thinking other than that of just emptying. This means that something else must come in addition. A disturbance can be there but I have this quiet place to meet the disturbance and have more contact with... or go in the direction of directing attention on the disturbance. Be present to the disturbance. This is the other method. The first one is to empty and the second one is to have something in addition. The other day I read that nothing can come into a cup when it is full. All right, that refers to the first method. Empty the cup and then fill it. But it doesn't refer to the fact that... it isn't true that nothing ever can come into a cup when it is full. Imagine having two cups that are sitting there in the kitchen sink. One of the cups, you pick it up and empty it. The other is stuck to the sink, so what you do is turn on the tap and begin to fill it so that what is in it is thinned out. This is a very clear picture of the second method. Are you with me? This is a very clear picture of this. Sometimes it is necessary to be sitting there and to be able to try to look at it.

B: I didn't understand what you meant when you said that the cup is stuck there.

A: For example, the cup is stuck in the emotional centre; you have a disturbance, yes? And you can't empty that cup, you can't get rid of that disturbance. You have the disturbance with you and then you can thin out what is in it through gradually filling it with something else. There is an energy that comes from being a witness. It is a witness's energy. It is in being a witness. *That* is where there is something. Yes?

B: That is what is so difficult for me to understand.

A: But you can't understand this until you experience it.

C: In order to thin it out, I have experienced that I have water with just so much dirt in the bottom of the bucket.

A: Yes.

C: And then I turn on the tap.

A: Yes.

C: And then I just let it overflow and slowly the dirty

water becomes more and more thinned out. And then it is almost clear...

A: Yes.

C: It gets thinner and thinner if you just let it stand there.

A: Yes.

C: So then it overflows and after awhile it is see-through.

A: Yes. Our problem is that we don't let the water run continuously. We have to let it run for a while, right? The second method of having something in addition – when it is interrupted then we are more concerned with taking away the disturbance. All the attention is drawn to the disturbance. You can imagine that you have just so much attention, measuring from zero to ten. If all of the attention is pulled to... the disturbance. All the attention goes to the disturbance. That is one situation. If you have some attention on the fact that you are being aware, then we have begun. There can be a relationship between being aware and being aware that you are aware. And that experience willingly mixes with a calmness already present in the body. That calmness in the body mixes willingly with that which is aware that you are aware. Or that which is a witness to the fact that you have directed attention on the disturbance... but what remains is to do it. *Then* you can understand. Right now I am only presenting an idea, it is only an idea, and then you can try it. You have a disturbance. You discover it. And then discover that there is someone that has discovered it, and in a way, yeah, try it. And have contact with... continue to know that you have discovered the disturbance, and then you begin to get closer. I think that this is all I can say on this right now. I can't get any closer by defining this idea. To get close is, after all, to do it. Is there anyone here that has a disturbance in the emotional centre now? Yes? All right. Well, take a look at that. Not just a little but continue, with attention and something else might come, perhaps? Have attention on the disturbance and divide the attention to include the fact that you know that you know about it. And then continue and listen to a question, or an observation if someone brings one up. Don't let go completely.

The advantage of dividing attention in more than two is that one of these, the disturbance, for example, will not have access to as much energy. This means that you can work indirectly by stifling the energy that goes to this "concern," this identification with the uneasiness. "I am not my uneasy emotional centre but I have an emotional centre which is uneasy due to different reasons. And I cannot be bothered right now to try to find out why. I might not be able to find out ever. And I am not really interested, not at the moment. I simply want to be aware of my uneasiness, here and now, and to try to verify this idea about filling the cup without emptying it."

We have an imaginary idea that freedom is not to have the disturbance, that isn't freedom. We must first be free from this idea and then gradually have a different type of experience. Freedom isn't so much not to have this or that, but to have an attitude to it that is preferable in relation to my aim. That is what it is about. In one way or another we have to experience this freedom, and we must also experience the way to it. It has to take a form in this form of existence. It has taken the form that there is often a disturbance in the emotional centre. We think it should be completely different, that we should not have it and that we should get rid of it, but the way to freedom isn't based on this type of thinking. That is an excluding attitude but it is possible to have a different...attitude.

SELECTED BIBLIOGRAPHY

Gurdjieff, G.I., *Beelzebub's Tales to his Grandson: All and Everything.*

Gurdjieff, G.I., *Meetings with Remarkable Men.*

Gurdjieff, G.I., *Life is only Real then when I Am.*

Ouspensky, P.D., *In Search of the Miraculous: Fragments of an Unknown Teaching.*

AUTHOR'S BIOGRAPHY

Terje Tonne (b. 1951)

Terje was educated as a Conservator at the Kent and McMint Fine Art Restorers in 1974. For the last 30 years he has had his own restoration studio where he has specialized in restoring fire and water damaged oil paintings for private collectors, museums and insurance companies. While studying in London in the early 70's he came across the Work ideas. He lives in Oslo, Norway and leads a group there along with his wife Ulrike.

To contact Den Norske Gurdjieff Stiftelsen, please use the following website:
www.gurdjieff-stiftelsen.no